D0257680

GALL IN THE DAY'S WORK

GALL

IN THE DAY'S WORK

THE WIT OF GLASGOW

CARTOONS BY

WILLIE GALL

COMMENTARY BY

CLIFF HANLEY

MAINSTREAM
PUBLISHING

The publishers wish to thank the *Evening Times*, who originally commissioned these cartoons, for their support and co-operation in the publication of this volume.

Copyright © Cartoons Willie Gall, 1989
© Text Cliff Hanley, 1989

All rights reserved

First published in Great Britain in 1989 by
MAINSTREAM PUBLISHING COMPANY (EDINBURGH) LTD
7 Albany Street, Edinburgh EH1 3UG

ISBN 1 85158 298 3 (cloth)

No part of this book may be reproduced or transmitted in any form or by any other means without the permission in writing from the publisher, except by a reviewer who wishes to quote brief passages in connection with a review written for insertion in a magazine, newspaper or broadcast.

British Library Cataloguing in Publication Data
Gall, Willie
    Gall in the day's work.
    1. Scottish humorous cartoons
    I. Title   II. Hanley, Clifford, *1922-*
    741.5'9411

ISBN 1-85158-298-3

Typeset in 12pt Imprint by Bookworm Typesetting Ltd., Edinburgh.
Printed in Great Britain by Richard Clay Ltd. Bungay, Suffolk.

CONTENTS

ON THE JOB

Adam started it, of course, and I refer not to eating the forbidden banana (nowhere does the Book of Genesis mention an apple, and my money is on the symbolic banana). He started working, and that is a very odd legacy to hand down to people who would rather just be ordinary millionaires and loaf about a lot.

Well, the old guy in Voltaire's *Candide* reckoned he had solved every philosophic problem when he said that people must cultivate their garden. Myself, I use an electric lawnmower on the window-box and that is as far as I mean to go.

In Glasgow, people have a love-hate relationship with work. They love to have a job, but they hate to actually do it. When I was a sub-editor in the old days, before such operatives bent over a word-processor and set up type electronically, we had copy-boys whose proud duty was to pick up the stories and bung them up a pneumatic tube to the compositors, who worked in hot metal (I could still eat the smell of that stuff). One of these lads spent all night hiding behind pillars to avoid actually doing anything useful. He must have been bored to death, but he felt he was achieving something. He was malingering.

Oh, a great game, malingering. It's a way of beating the System. It takes it out of you, of course, and while you're hiding behind pillars you're liable to find your mind wandering into the meaning of meaning, and the fact that you're an incurable plook, and that women don't fancy you a lot, and that you're developing a wart on your nose. But you're beating the System.

Your workmates, running their legs down to the kneecaps, have no time for depressing introspection, and they look quite happy, the dreary young finks. They are the victims of the System.

Yes, we are schizophrenic about work in Glasgow, and let's face it, having two heads is more fun than one. We created the Industrial Revolution, didn't we? And when we got it, we didn't fancy it a lot. I mean, working shifts and getting dirty fingers and being covered night and day with soot.

So. We fret about the prospect of being unemployed. In my schooldays, redundancy meant a clumsy use of the language, a repetition, like saying a tall giant or a greedy glutton. Another word for the error was pleonasm, but let's not go into that – my brain is suddenly exhausted.

Now, redundancy means a working man being thrown on the scrapheap because a multinational has found something else to do with the multi-million subsidy it got from the British Government to create jobs; spend it on a trip to the Costa Brava, probably.

When Billy Connolly decided to go for performing full-time, his father was terrified of the insecurity it meant. After all, the boy had a steady job in a shipyard, fixed for life. Aye, that'll be right, as they keep saying in Govan.

We don't take the job as seriously as we used to. If we can be persuaded to pause for a minute from filling in the coupon, and look back through history, we do tend to get a wee bit cynical about the city's splendid record in creating industry and jobs.

Probably the only profession with a secure future is working down the sewers, because we'll always need sewers. Unfortunately, I myself have spent a brief period down there, crawling backward and pulling water and stuff towards me to keep everything flowing. Being a Stakhanovite by nature, I pulled quite hard and produced a tidal wave that filled my chest-high oilskins with stinking stuff. When I got home, my wife burned all my clothes and forbade me ever to stand near a stank again. So I no longer have any job security, and boy, am I glad of that.

Yes, we are in two minds about work, and I am glad I gave it up thirty years ago. I deeply admire my neighbours racing to catch the 8.25 every morning in life, but like many Glaswegians, I am a mere spectator, agreeing with Mark Twain, who said, "Work fascinates me. I could look at it all day long."

Well, let's be serious, if you can stand that. It's a tough life having to work. And it's a tough life having not to work. We need a job to keep us out from under the wife's feet, especially if the wife wears high-heeled shoes. Do I sound sexist? Right enough, the wife may well be taking her high heels out to do her part-time bit and giving our spines a wee rest.

We are what we do, as well as what we think. On the job then, and make Glasgow great. Or off the job, and make Glasgow grate. Workers of the world, unite, if you can rustle up enough fellow-workers to organise a meeting in a phone box. Redundants of the world, unite, and then wonder why you bothered.

It is all very confusing, and if it isn't, I have failed somewhere. But The Job is a big thing in Glasgow, even if it's only a distant memory for some people. And we're very good at it. Well, at least we're very good at thinking about it. Let us sit and think about it. Or, in some cases, let us just sit, and let Willie Gall think about it.

"Brothers, we find ourselves in an impossible situation
... they've went an' gave in to all wur demands."

"It's a Sunday BAN we've been asking for on the ferries, Chentlemen."

"Whit's up, shortage o' dust?"

"As the owner of a British Telecom share I'm orderin'
ye oot o' ma phone box."

"Any day now it'll be askin' for a three day week and an index- linked pension."

"Whit are they playin' fur openers, Jimmy, Beethoven's Unfinished?"

"Big deal! Ah'll still huv tae rise an' answer the door when the postman brings it"

"Haw, Wullie, is ma take-home pay the wan the boss gies me or the wan Ah gie the wife?"

"Haw, Jimmy ... ah've got two consultants, how many huv you got?"

"OK, ye've got the job an' now ye can join the pickets at the gate an' prevent yersel' fae startin'."

"Has it ever occurred to you, Arthur, that we've been living off it for years?"

"So whit's new? The coonter Ah go tae is always closed."

"Ah suppose we'd better take a wee walk doon an' tell the fire brigade!"

"What is it this time, a conference, a seminar, a symposium, a convention, a talk-in, a congress or jist a meetin'?"

"How dae thae expect us tae hear wur transistor wi' a' this racket goin' oan?"

"Now that I'm selling ice-cream, Morag, I hope the place doesn't become another Blackpool!"

"Ah've been advocatin' that fur years."

"When Ah asked the shop steward whit he wiz daein aboot rubbish he said he wis jist talkin' it as usual."

"Ah say there should be a differential between me an' him that's only been coming here fur ten year!"

"An' whit dae we get fur a' the extra effort?"

"Naw, Wullie, fur hivven's sake, Wullie, ye're no' suposed tae dae that, Wullie!"

"If their timekeeping's normal that should start about the fourth o' September."

"As economies must be made, we'll have to employ another 300 people to make out the necessary 250 redundancy notices."

"Whit does escalate mean, Brian?"

"Are you sure he's one of us?"

"He refuses tae accept redundancy."

"Wakin' up, Jimmie, ye're wanted at a meetin' as a representative from the shop floor."

"I suppose that means we're back to cold, dirty trains running late."

"Don't think o' this train bein' hauf an' hour late, Missus, just imagine ye're oan the next wan two hours early."

"Simple, i'ntit! We've got thoosan's o' unemployed an' Ah'm wan o' the nucleus!"

THE GEMME

It usually all starts with a ball of some kind, though this is not always essential in modern rugby, in which an upturned face is often preferred.

Traditionally, the first ball was a jaurie or bool, sometimes mistakenly referred to as a marble by ignorant foreigners. It is worth recalling this mania, and the curious fact that there was a jaurie season. Nobody announced it, it just arrived and suddenly everybody was mad for the things. Out of season, it was taboo. Weird.

Basic variations included linie, for which a straight line was scratched on the surface of the back court and the winner was the brat who could roll his bools nearest it. Sometimes a circle was preferred. Moshie was the real game, of course, with three holes arranged in a triangle and a set of rules that would have baffled a Philadelphia lawyer. When we moved to another back court we took the holes with us.

The basic bool was a wally sphere, and glessies, though pretty with their internal spiral patterns, were considered a bit jessie. The killer was the plunker cast in lead, or sometimes a giant ball-bearing.

On the way to and from school, bools were scooshed along the gutter in pursuit of one another, and when a strike looked imminent there would be urgent cries, like "Nae sheevies!" (Sheevie: a simple rolling motion) and "Big pots!" or "Wee pots!" and "Three spangs an' a knucklie!"

This was all a preliminary training for booting or heiding a ball, and if there was no tanner ba' available, a daud of rolled-up newspaper bound with string did the trick. Then there was the weird madness of wee heidies, where a young loonie faced the close wall and tried to bounce a tanner ba' between it and his forehead a million times. Old-time champs at this can still be identified by the hemispherical dents in the middle of the broo.

A touch of viciousness crept in with the game of King, a form of tig in which you didn't touch your quarry but hurled a ball at his skull; or her skull, which was even more fun. The equivalent of prehistoric man clubbing prehistoric woman to show he fancied her. No doubt many a tender romance started with a circular bruise on the jaw.

Cricket, though an alien pursuit, had its fans. But nobody could afford stumps, of course. They had to be chalked on a back wall, which had the advantage that no bowler could send your bails flying, and most of the match was a screaming argument about whether the ball had hit the chalk marks or just the bricks.

Tennis was something else. It took a bold and brazen male teenager to be seen walking to the park with a racquet, because his scruffy contemporaries reckoned he was a pansy, and said so. Aye, a pansy game. McEnroe may be a lot of things, but I would hesitate to call him a pansy to his face.

The same with hockey, of course. A lassie sport. I played it at school because I was a six-stone weakling and you can really get the boak being charged from both sides by fifteen-stone escaped murderers. The incredible hulks sneered at this, but when they condescended to join us for a laugh they discovered the grim fact that the hockey stick is the great equaliser, especially in the hands of somebody my height.

Apart from sitting on a horse, which was okay – the riding school guy tried to persuade me to become a jockey – I never had much interest in the Sport of Kings, and I know why. A guy on the inside put me on to a rank outsider that was going to be a cert at 100-1. I tracked down the local bookie's runner in the boozer and tried to put my lot on it. He gave me a long fatherly lecture on how gambling had ruined his life, he wasn't going to let it ruin mine, and he was doing me a favour by refusing the bet. It won by three lengths and the experience put me right off.

When it comes to adult soccer, I'm neutral – I thought Mo Johnston manufactured baby powder. My only contact with the game is my standing order on the treble chance, in which I don't even need to know the teams' names, because they have abandoned them in favour of numbers.

Golf remains the ultimate self-inflicted wound for the ordinary punter, like the American on a tee at St Andrews who was told fiercely by a greenkeeper that it was compulsory to put his ball on a peg. "This is my fourth shot," he bleated.

The important thing about any gemme is that it is absolutely useless. It can't solve the balance of payments crisis, or the housing problem, or burst pipes, or week-long queues at airports. But think of the really useful things we can do: clearing choked drains, going to the dentist, paying the poll tax, changing a flat tyre in a blizzard, digging up dandelions. When we ponder on these noble tasks, we suddenly realise that the gemme is truly the gemme.

"The Olympic ideal, my son, is tae prove that people can run quick withoot bein' chased by the polis."

"Haw, Jimmy! Gonny gie us a light, Jimmy?"

"Ah bet the old adrenalin's bashin' away like the clappers, Mrs Alexander."

"See this.... If it wisnae fur thae dampt fags ye wid be playin' fur Scotland."

"Ah think that band on his heid must be too tight or somethin'."

"Ah sometimes wonder if the hauf o' thur teams is even TRYIN' tae draw!"

"Speakin' as an atheist that supports Stenhousemuir Ah couldnae care less."

"So ye've cried him efter eleeven fitba' players! It's a guid thing yer man's no' a rugby supporter!"

"Coincidence that, you an' Sandy Lyle no' being in the Ryder Cup Team!"

"Wur priorities this year is no' tae win leagues or cups but tae huv a fancier strip than the rest o' them."

"Why could we no' be sponsored by a beer firm or somethin'?"

"If ye ask me that yin jist scores goals so that he'll get kissed an' cuddled!"

"His personal best at the last Olympics wis eighteen lagers, sixty fags an' ten bags o' crisps in wan day."

"Ah don't fancy huvin' tae curse an' swear at the referee on Sundays, dae you Brian?"

"Ah got a sponsor fur the new season."

"Me an' yer dad disnae believe in drink, son, so promise ye'll just throw liminade bottles!"

"Honest, it's no' fur drinkin', it's jist fur throwin' oan tae the park."

"How many cans o' beer does that represent?"

"When the fitba's feenished are we gonna be cricket hooligans or tennis hooligans?"

"See ma man! Since he heard that a Clergyman won the pools he turns his collar back tae front when he posts his coupon!"

"Ah admit Ah've had hundred's o' gifts but they've a' been pairs o' specs."

"He's got a terrible problem – he wants tae be a hooligan but he hates fitba'!"

"Fur your kind o' money Ah'm willin' tae forget Ah'm a Partick Thistle supporter."

"I think it's diabolical – if there's wan thing ma Darren hates it's chuckin' beer cans fae a sittin' position."

"He gets his excercise fae watchin' athletics oan the telly."

"Aye, Mrs Wulson got flung oot the bingo last night fur huvin' hauf-a-dozen Valium in her handbag."

"Ah fancy Seve Ballesteros an' Ah'm no' talkin' aboot golf."

"The lady is now twenty-seven over par goin' tae the fourth."

"Ladies are requested not to follow the World Cup custom of swapping jerseys after the game."

"Blast it, Fiona, one can't walk down the street in one's kilt without being pestered aboot black market tickets for Wembley."

"An' that's him jist goin' hame tae watch it on the telly."

"Let's face it, fifty years supportin' Partick Thistle disnae automatically entitle ye tae an O.B.E."

"That, my son, is David Coleman receiving the gold medal fir hysterics."

"Nae fitba', so he's away tae the World Chess Championship at Reykjavik!"

"Ah widnae huv thought a Wimbledon ticket tout wid dae much trade at Parkheid Cross."

"As Ah've nae heid for heights dae yiz mind if Ah jist run aboot blawin' a wee whistle?"

"It disnae huv tae be a good yin. It's jist tae throw oan the flerr when Ah'm angry!"

"Good auld Wimbledon! It's the only time Ah hear love mentioned in this hoose!"

"Ah think he done very well tae come in second."

"An' remember, when we're showin' the gemme tae them next door it's ca'd backgammon no' biled ham!"

"Don't forget, son, Ah'll want ma claes rope back fur Monday."

"Ye wid huv somethin' tae say if ah watched seven hours o' fitba every day."

"If ye eat yer dinner ye'll grow up tae be a big strong man like thae Russian lady weight throwers!"

"Must be Royal Ascot time again."

"When are they bringin' oot that anti-blood sports Bill?"

"Whit d'ye mean chappin'? Ye canny be chappin' at bridge."

"Whar's yer loneliness o' the long distance runner noo?"

"Buildin' an extension tae house a' thae olympic gold medals, Ah expect."

"Nae wonder ye're whacked.... Ye wisnae supposed tae run there an' back."

"The joggin' seems tae be a' the go nooadays."

"Ah canny see Scientology replacin' this, can you Margaret?"

"Ah wid lock up a' thae skinheads fur a kick-off."

"We've got snooker on the telly, darts on the telly, why no' dominoes on the telly?"

"Right! Any union member that does meters too quick is in fur a drugs test."

STAYING ALIVE

We have all met the man who complained to the doctor that he had practically lost the ability to walk, and was told gently that he had put both legs down one trouser. Strange ailments await us wherever we tread, or fail to tread.

And imaginary ailments are just as scary as real ones, because we live inside our skulls and the wee grey cells can drive us up the wall. There is an evil true tale of the new boy at Glasgow Customs office in the days when the bowler was *sine qua non*, and obligatory forbye. He got himself togged up at Dunn's, with his initials inside and everything, and felt like a film star.

His evil elders checked on his hat size and privately bought another three sizes bigger, with initials, and swopped them. At closing time, the victim proudly put on the hat, over his eyes, whipped it off and walked out carrying it. Next morning he arrived with the band stuffed with paper. The swines stuffed his rightful hat with paper and swopped again.

This went on for days until he turned up missing and his mother phoned to say he was at the doctor to have his head examined for some dread disease unknown to medical science.

The rest of us get by on milder phobias, like the conviction that we're shrinking. Stop worrying about that. We are.

You can worry about being overweight if you're looking for a hobby. The Romans had the trick for that. They gorged themselves to the gullet, then took an emetic and disposed of the lot. It is not to be recommended unless you see it as a pagan ritual and you're into pagan rituals. And what does overweight mean? Rubens and his mates fancied lassies with a high inflation count, and I have heard tall, skinny girls being advised to keep their legs crossed when near a stank. But we're not all meant to be the same shape, and the scenery would be dreary if we were.

So, being healthy can be nothing more than a state of mind. Some people getting older realise that their minds are going because they can't remember the name of somebody they met twenty years ago in Rothesay, and even quite fancied (in certain weather in Rothesay, people can fancy anybody). They don't realise that the bloke next door has never been able to remember the name of his brother, and feels quite good about it.

Some people spend their days and nights fretting about their diet and what it is going to do to their grandchildren. Others get tore into the turnips for every meal and have musical burps, or rifts, as they were called before we heard of the Radio Doctor (who got old and died, by the way).

Everything we do will affect our health. Smoking, drinking, not smoking, not drinking. A studious keelie made the momentous discovery that, contrary to popular belief, booze is a depressant and fags are a stimulant. It changed his life. Now he does both simultaneously, to preserve a mental balance.

Standing up can be bad for us. Sitting down can be bad for us. Lying down can be bad for us, especially in the wrong company. Hivvings, what are we to do about it? In the Middle Ages you could have your limbs falling off if somebody put the evil eye on you. Today the villains can't afford specs and we're safe.

The answer is simple. We keep the heid. By all means go to the doctor when you have a weird feeling in the small of your back. The doctor wants to know about it, because he is desperate to tell you about his own weird feeling on the inside of his right ankle. If you feel bold, you can prescribe something for him, like a pair of socks without a killer crab inside one of them. Then let him whip up your shirt and discover a nest of ants in your semmit.

The comforting thing is that the medical profession never stops. It introduced us to germs, and then viruses, and then psychosomatic insanities, and salmonella, and it is beginning to fancy wild jags in the form of acupuncture, and maybe hypnotism, or juggling, or whatever comes up next, as the Romans might have said after a banquet.

The more we get from the docs, the less likely it is that we will ever die, and hooray for that. Unfortunately, it means that yon Mrs McCafferty next door will never die either. So maybe we should all get a wee bit seeck. It's a nice hobby.

"It says 'Jimmy Smith disnae need glasses'."

"If ma Uncle Andra wis alive the day he wid tell ye smokin' 60 a day never did him nae herm."

"Come on, Tam, ye'll need tae smoke quicker than that if Ah've tae get this fur coat!"

"A rerr crop o' tomatoes, Ah think it's got somethin' tae dae wi' this greenhouse effect they're talkin' aboot."

"As we're very busy this morning the doctor says would the hypochondriacs wait till the last."

"When this ceases to be a private bed surely it won't become known as a public one!"

"How dae they expect us tae get better when wur flamin' get-well cards is held up in the post?"

"Ah'm off ma food, doctor, could ye gie me something tae keep me that way?"

"At least it's nice tae know ye're an' ancillary worker an' no' a skivvy!"

"Right! The first wan tae make a funny joke aboot bed pans gets flung oot!"

"See this flamin' hassle in the Health Service. It'll serve them right if people refuse tae become no' weel."

"Typical.... No' content wi' ordinary Legionnaire's disease you've got tae take French Foreign Legionnaire's disease."

"But Ah only volunteered tae come in an' wash the dishes."

"Ah wonder whit flamin' genius decided peelin' **spuds** an' polishin' **flairs** wis the cure fur appendicitis an' a double hernia."

"On yer road hame call in at the health food **store** an' ask for ma money back."

"Ah can appreciate the need fur doublin' up, doctor, but does it always need tae be wi' the same sex?"

"You will realise, of course, that because of industrial action we have to call on such members of staff as are available."

"That's a' the thanks Ah get fur devotin' the best years o' ma life tae bein' no' weel."

"And we have a selection of 'get-well' cards for dissatisfied customers!"

"It amounts to this, darling, if I can't be ill privately I shall refuse to be ill at all."

"Ah'm worried because Ah huvnae enough money tae pay yer bill!"

"Huv yiz onything tae luft a nasal blockade?"

"What d'you mean, old boy, *you've* got a drink problem?"

"Seein' as you are ma new doctor Ah've made a tape o' ma ailments."

"You're lucky wi' yer temperature o' a hundred an' two, Wullie, it's freezin' cauld ootside."

"Dae Ah take this before or efter meals, Doctor?"

"Ah'm beginnin' tae stock-pile Valium, whit are you beginnin' tae stock-pile?"

"That's the tenth flamin' case this week o' politician's door-chappin' knuckles."

"Feel terrible, doctor.... Ah think Ah must huv went an' flexed ma roster"

"Right, Mrs McCallum, you are now immunised against Typhoid, Cholera, Smallpox, Malaria, Beri-Beri and Whooping Cough.... Have a nice holiday in Tighnabruaich."

"Comin' here wance a week ye begin tae run oot o' symptoms, sure ye dae?"

"Not to worry, Mr Arbuthnot, anyone who ISN'T feeling depressed these days I refer to a psychiatrist."

"Right! Sunstrokes first, skint backs next an' sweat rashes over therr."

"Put it this way, old chap, you've failed your M.O.T."

"A common motorist's complaint these day, I'm afraid, over-gritted teeth caused by driving on under-gritted roads.

"See thur teeth that went up? Well, they've fell doon!"

"Ah'll put ye on tae these anti-depression tablets, they cured me."

"So you're a bit off colour.... What colour would you like to be?"

"Wi' a' this extra money they should be able tae gie the likes o' me an' you a season ticket."

"Ah don't mind ye bein' a hypochondriac but dae ye hav tae be a bed ridden **hypochondriac?**"

"Terrible bad back, Ah think Ah'll huv tae go tae wan o' thae Disc Jockeys!"

"It's anither starvin' tobacconist wantin' a hand-out."

"It has really taken a' the pleasure oot o' bein' no' well."

"OK! OK! Ye can start smokin' again."

"Of course, I blame Sir Walter Raleigh for bringing it into the country in the first place."

"Whit d'ye mean ye're on a Youth Trainin' Scheme fur surgeons?"

"Ah reckon ye've tae be no' weel aboot twice a week tae get yer money's worth."

"Ah think this pair'll be a'right, son."

"See ma nerves! See prescriptions! Ah wish somebody wid start a Valiums Anonymous."

"Ah sprained ma wrist openin' 'get-well' cards."

"Put it this way.... You're so much under par you could be leading the field in the Glasgow Golf Classic."

'That's a' we flamin' well need, a ward fu' o' protesters wi' pnuemonia."

"Ye realise, of course, that wance the grub's privatised ye'll be expected tae leave a tip under the plate."

"Do you agree that nurses should be better paid, Mr Thompson?"

"The wife says it's Lumbaga but Ah'd like a second opinion!"

"Ah don't know whit's worst, ma Athlete's Foot or ma Tennis Elba!"

"Hamstring trouble.... Swallowed a bit wi' his breakfast."

"The wife's comin' in the day again. Ah sometimes wish they wid let oot their visitin' hours tae private contractors."

"He's been oan the Valium since he heard there wis mair joabs comin' tae Scotland."

An' Ah don't agree wi' them killin' coos so that we can eat big steaks – that's why Ah jist want hauf a pun' o' mince."

"Ah'll tell ye how bad conditions are fur nurses.... They eat a' wur grapes an' drink a' wur Lucozade."

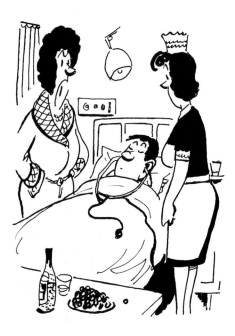

"Helluva state o' affairs when Ah come back fae the bathroom tae find a junior doctor sleepin' in ma bed."

"Ah canny come oot, Mrs Wulson, Ah've got a' ma thermal underwear wrapped roon' the watter pipes."

"Aye, they say it's a' comin' through that big hole in the ozone layer."

"Ah wonder how much that is we'll get each if we stop."

"Look! Ah've been walkin' on *roads* wi' high tar content a' ma life an' it hasnae done me nae harm!"

"OK! OK! Environmental pollution upsterrs, Mac!"

"Haw, Wullie, gee's a haulf an' a pint o' Lucozade."

"They should gie ye a month's notice aboot that kind o' thing."

"As Ah always say, Agnes, it's the quality of life that coonts!"

"A guid touch o' frost'll soon put a stop tae that nonsense!"

"Of course, Ah blame the environment. We never had a' this trouble before the environment was inventit!"

"The pollution's that bad there's hardly a place left tae throw doon an empty beer can!"

GET THE POLIS

We live in a law-abiding country, where in many areas a woman can walk the streets at night and come home quite disappointed. We live in a sink of iniquity where people don't only break through our windows, they take the windows home with them to organise a bit of double glazing.

 See crime? Well, now and then you can. It was different in the old days, when there was none, and we could all sleep cheerfully in our beds, bugs and all, without even locking the door. Ah, the peaceful old days of yore, the days of Jack the Ripper and Doctor Pritchard and Cain. Things have gone to pigs and whistles since Cain. I mean, he only knocked off his brother in a fit of pique and then went East of Eden to set up gambling dens and establish the profit-making society.

 The difference really is that in Cain's time there were no polis. If there had been, one of them might well have intervened to point out that the boy had no licence for that. For that dagger, or airgun, or whatever – we don't know how he did it. Anyway, he fetched up in the land of Nod, where many of us do quite regularly, and got married, and had weans, and possibly belted them about a lot. Why didn't the Garden of Eden, and the land of Nod, for that matter, have a few polis available?

 Our polis don't actually abolish crime, but they bother us when we are slipping a screwdriver into the gas meter and may well discourage us from sawing down the Kingston Bridge. They are not perfect, of course, which makes them totally acceptable because we are not perfect either. I am, but we are not.

 There was a poster in a lot of banks a few years ago showing a bobby racing up a garden path, and the caption read, "Thank goodness they're here." On one sheet, some irreverent swine had written, "Now we can *ALL* get beaten up." Well, they vary, like the rest of us. Some of them aren't even tall any more, and when the height requirement was reduced, journalists started talking about mini-cops, until I myself insisted they should return to pure standard English and call the fellows wee toty polis.

They get younger all the time, of course. Some of them even get Younger, others prefer Tennent's. They are human, whatever people may say. A few months back, three of them in plain clothes all tried to arrest one another, and that at least shows they were dedicated to the job. We are all entitled to make a citizen's arrest, but apart from the odd delinquent collie mongrel, I wouldn't recommend it, and even the collie might be a detective-inspector with a long wig.

But we manage to live together. The polisman has a good idea that the rest of us are all potential criminals, because he himself at the age of six once nipped a wee lassie's bum in a fit of sheer savagery and knows what the human race is about. He might even have nicked a sweetie snowball from the Tally's, and learned that man is vile and all that kind of rubbish.

All right. We put up with him. He puts up with us. We have no option.

There is something very comforting about the sight of the blue uniform. Society, for all its madness, is under control. The man in the uniform may of course be just a security guard, planning to skip the country with a million quid, but there's a nice solid look to him, and always the chance that he might ask us to help him pedal his tandem on the way to Brazil.

Let us be grateful for the boys in blue. And let us have a close handy when we see one in the distance.

**"If they want everybody tae wear seat-belts they'll huv
tae gie us a' motor caurs, sure they will?"**

"Ah'm all for a bit o' atmosphere, but hirin' a big polis
tae obstruct the view is, in my opinion, overdoin' it."

"It's no' fair, Sarge, you got switchin' oan the siren yesterday an' ye said it wid be ma turn the day."

"D'ye mind if Ah blow it up he's been drinkin'?"

"How can Ah be a bad example tae ma family when Ah'm in here a' the time?"

"You young people have a glamorous tradition to uphold; Dixon of Dock Green, Z Cars, Softly Softly, The Sweeney, The Bill . . ."

"Ah'm no' protestin' against nuthin', mate! Ah fell!"

"Whit d'ye mean 'no comment,?"

"That's our new plain clothes man!"

"By the way, if ye get the job ye're no' usin' ma best clothes rope."

"Is this whit ye mean by closer community links?"

"Fitba'? Naw, we're goin' tae the Edinburgh Festival."

"Are you in charge of this cycle, madame?"

"The prisoner refuses to appear, your lordship – says he's on dock strike!"

"Ah didnae mind bein' in the cage but the bird seed gave me indigestion."

"Excuse me askin', but huv yiz got smokin' an' non-smokin' cells?"

"That's him!"

"Jist ma luck tae suffer fae kleptomania AND claustrophobia."

"He's oan your side, he throws bottles an' beer cans at footba' hooligans."

"They say it's a sign ye're gettin' auld when the neds begin tae look young."

"Ah wis jist tryin' tae relieve the overcrowdin' yiz are aye moanin' aboot."

"Ah want tae lodge a complaint aboot police brutality."

"OK, if ye're no' launderin' money why the washin' machine in the back shoap?"

"How is it women polis on the telly are always smashers, Agnes?"

"Ah only come because Ah love bein' shoved aboot by a big polis."

"If it's only consolation ye're no' bein' luftit, ye're bein impeached?"

CELEBRATE OR ELSE

The simple act of wakening up every morning in Glasgow is a kind of celebration. For many citizens it is a big surprise celebration, like "Jings, ah'm alive!" The murky memories of the previous night make this an improbable bonus.

Well, we have to celebrate *something*. Breathing is a good excuse, since we can think of mates who gave it up and have nothing much left to celebrate. Mind you, Mark Twain or somebody once said that no good can come of a day that starts with getting up. But with any luck, and a lot of courage, we can survive that trauma, and get tore into accepting life, which gets better as the afternoon wears off.

In ancient Rome, they had the Saturnalia, a week when the aristocrats changed places with the slaves, and the proles had a whale of a time doing whatever they fancied to whomever they fancied. We don't need that in Glasgow, because we do it in our skulls 52 weeks in the year – and it actually works better in your skull.

But we accept the need for periodic bits of nonsense. Easter, when you roll eggs, can be very frustrating if you have picked up a scrambled egg, but we persevere.

The Glasca Ferr has dwindled a bit. It used to be okay, the factories were shut and you could actually see the sky for a fortnight, through occasional holes in the rain layer, and everybody shot down the Clyde on paddle steamers, ignoring the weather and trooping below decks to look at the engines, which seemed to consist of optic measures. Well, times change, and the Ferr is now staggered. Again. It is regularly celebrated with the ritual of sleeping on an airport floor for a week, brushing up on the Spanish for "Dos Bacardis por favor, Jimmy."

The exact date of St Andrew's Night keeps escaping me, because around November I am still wondering what became of the September Weekend. Was it in Malaga I tripped over that drunken polis, or Machrinhanish?

Well, but. Mean to say. Christmas, annat, eh? We don't have to be too religious to recognise that Christmas is the game. The tree, the fairy lights, the wee electric trains – they are an ancient tradition. They must have gone a bomb in ancient Jerusalem.

It can be fraught, mind you, when you discover that the wee toy aeroplane you put in the wife's sock last year has mysteriously turned up in your sock this year. It's even worse when you don't notice the thing at all and think your left toes have gone lame because the jaggy wee thing is still in there as you hirple to the out-patients' department and brood on death. But that is all a bit of the fun, isn't it? Depending on how you define fun.

And never mind, Hogmanay is hovering. The night when you will discover you love everybody, and sometimes forget to keep your hands off them, and waken up on the fourth of January wondering what became of your teeth.

Certainly, Scotland gave Hogmanay to the world, and even remote countries like England have cottoned on to the tradition, so that neighbours from down south will appear in the sma' oors offering a handful of dross and looking for a huge free booze-up. They tend to sing Old Lang Syne as well.

The Burns suppers follow quite soon after that. Nothing can force me to say a word about Burns suppers. Away and invent a celebration of your own. It is all too exhausting. And what's this jaggy thing I keep feeling in my sock?

"They bring religion intae Christmas an' noo they're tryin' tae dae the same wi' Easter."

"Whit d'ye mean, ye jist want snakes an' ladders?"

"Ah think we've got a gate-crasher."

"Well, how is it ah can face Hogmanay withoot a flamin trainin' schedule."

"Ye're gettin nae crisps this year, the price is diabolical!"

"How is it we're huvin' cauld turkey when we only had mince on Christmas Day?"

"Huv you an' yer computer no' finished yer office party yet?"

"By the way, we're huvin' duck this year.... Ah throw a tin o' spam an' you duck."

"Nooadays ye go tae the theatre tae get AWAY fae the pantomime!"

"Ah don't expect an auld geezer like you'll huv heard o' computer games."

"See ma man! This is the thirty-fifth year in succession he husnae gave me a fur coat fur ma Christmas."

"Ah'm jist sendin' beggin' letters this year."

"And what, may I ask, is wrong with getting your Christmas present a day or two late?"

"He's gettin' a new transistor an' Ah'm gettin' new ear plugs!"

"This year we're jist pourin' Brandy ower a Chinese carry-oot an' settin' fire tae it."

"Terrible tae think that there's only twenty-odd shopliftin' days left tae Christmas, i'ntit, Mrs Wulson."

"An' don't give us that auld stuff aboot a balance o' payments crisis!"

"We've had roast turkey, cauld turkey, minced turkey, turkey rissoles.... D'ye fancy turkey an' custard?"

"I suppose I can take it that you are not affected by inflation, the falling pound or other financial considerations!"

"If onybody mentions first-footin' Ah'll probably go intae hysterics."

"A' ye've did since Ne'erday is sit there an' moan aboot the price o' Asprins."

"Ye asked us tae bring a bottle.... Ah canny wait tae see whit ye're goin' tae put in it."

"Can't promise anything, of course, but after Christmas we'll try to get you fixed up in the Youth Opportunity Programme."

"This is a carry-oot for a carry-oan tae carry-ower tae Ne'erday – Merry Christmas!"

"Can ye imagine whit Christmas must huv been like before credit cards?"

"Ah've jist came in tae apologise fur the Happy New Year Ah wished yiz."

RIGHT LEFT AND CENTRE

An Englishman – and Jimmie, we have to watch them – once said that the political instrument could not create human happiness. His name was E.M. Forster, and he wrote *A Passage to India* as well. My own response was that he should have taken that passage and kept out of here.

Crivvens, and jings, and various other classical allusions. We know, or at least we knew, that politics was hovering there to create the ideal society. At sixteen, I had given the subject a total study, and let me tell you, or youse, I knew everything. Oh, what a time of life. Being a staunch keelie, I had joined the revolutionary left wing. Ugh, I regret leaving that, because today I know practically nothing, every morning I am more iggerant than I was the day before. It was great.

Come the big change, which might well be the next Tuesday at three o'clock sharp, the world would be transformed, and even different. We would all be tall and handsome, or petite and gorgeous, able to speak French and Russian and Esperanto and totally irresistible to the other sex, whatever they might be. Ah. French. Vive la difference, Hughie, or Hughina as the case may be, here goes.

In the meantime, we worked like maniacs to get our spokesmen into the Cooncil, or Parliament, or wherever. The fact that some of them had a lot of bother with the English language was irrelevant, or even irrevelant, in their pronunciation. Once they were working in the Municipal Buildings, they would be the people of the future, and that lassie with the maroon bike would rush to my arms.

Aye, okay, the maroon bike would have gone well with ma roon shooders.

It didn't *exactly* work out like that. Our heroes still talked about the Municipal Buildings, and in succeeding years some of them visited Barlinnie and asked for extended accommodation.

Okay, see politics? We are none of us perfect, except me, and even I have been known to pick my nose when I thought nobody was looking. That lassie with the maroon bike was looking, of course.

So we had our outstanding choices, failing to speak French or anything else worth hearing, and sort of messing about and getting nice chuck and booze at the City Chambers, and even I hadn't shot up to six feet. I had been cheated.

But they get on with the job. I know now that I don't have much idea of what the job is. It's about holding on to the job, I suppose, because it looks a lot better than working down a sewer. I have worked down a sewer and it is not very glamorous, though it's probably a lot more hygienic than politics. So they stick in there, and tell us the tale, and luckily, we usually ignore it. So we voted for this chap, because he was there at the time. But the keelie system is that you vote for him, and from the minute he's in, you're against him.

We have inherited a tradition from Imperial Rome, or pinched it, which is more like us. When a new senator entered the chamber, he made a show of fighting like a tiger against being installed, and had to be forcibly dragged to the bench to accept the honour. This showed that he was convinced he was not worthy of the honour.

The same thing happens in the House of Commons. I mean, if the guy actually wanted power, he would be the kind of guy who was unfit for it. So he finally submits to force majeure, if I can lapse into Esperanto. The voters know he is a plook all the same, and in Glasgow we have slightly less than a total reverence for our elected representatives.

We're not actually daft.

"See that! That's magic! Ah love bananas."

"Absolutely astounding, darling. She was able to tell me that I'm a Conservative and that I'm here for some kind of conference."

"Whit's the bettin' he puts up capital gains tax jist when ah'm floggin' the auld chist o' drawers in ma kitchen?"

"The Scots, of course, don't know there's anything south of Watford."

"Ah don't vote fur naebody, Jimmie, Ah've jist came on the tap deck fur a smoke."

"A' we need noo's the drug testin' equipment."

"See a' that bother aboot the Satanic Verses, thank hivvens he didnae write the chorus as well."

"Ah'll be votin' for the first wan that admits they're jist wantin' intae Europe fur the cheap booze an' the sunshine."

"Control yer greenfly, Jimmie?"

"There's a vote catcher if ever Ah saw wan."

"D'ye think Ah could have ma cheese toasted on a nice wee slice o' bread, dear?"

"Haw, Jimmy, who's that dampt chancer again ye said Ah wisnae tae vote fur?"

"Huv ye decided yet whether or no' ye're goin' tae pay the Poll Tax, Walter?"

"Anything aboot it bein' compulsory fur M.P.s an' Toon Cooncilors?"

"Don't tell me they're privatisin' Parliament."

"The word democracy, my son, means that everybody's wrang except yersel'."

"I always thought microphones were invented tae SAVE people fae shoutin'"

"Tae announce that she's standin' for president in fower years' time, Ah expect."

"Of course, if it came tae proportional representation you wid huv three votes tae his wan."

"Me an' her baith."

It'll soon be time fur us tae stop smokin' an' drinkin' again."

"You'll find the Party Manifestos under 'Fiction', sir."

"Ye might find this hard tae believe, son, but Ah'm a floater!"

"Ah wonder when they'll get roon' tae fresh air an' daylight."

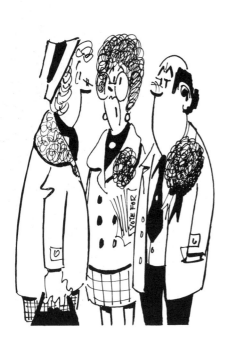

"He's no' too far tae the right an' he's no' too far tae the left an' he's no' quite in the middle.... As a matter o' fact he's loast."

"Ye could hardly ca' it a Military Coup jist because wur new cooncillor's a captain in the Boy's Brigade!"

"How dae ye expect tae advance the cause o' world peace goin' on a demo dressed like that?"

"Nae problem, if fags, booze an' petrol goes up we'll be savin' it by no' paying wur Poll Tax."

"It's an opinion poll to establish your opinion about opinion polls."

"We're certainly gettin' plenty o' practice!"

"The best thing aboot a Party Conference is the Conference Party."

"An' next week there'll be a new M.P. in Westminster scratchin' his heid an' tryin' tae remember whit promises he made in Hillhead."

"Not that far forward, Margaret, not that far forward!"

"Daft week fur a holiday in Brighton, they'll think we're either Tories or polis."

"One has to keep such a low profile hat-wise in case one up-stages Margaret!"

"The Budget, my son, is what people watched before they had video nasties."

"Ah'm no' goin' tae huv ma man governed by a wumman!"

"How's that fur comfort an' joy? Wur safety in the hands o' Reagan an' his pals."

"Noo that Govan's hoachin' wi' T.V. cameras Ah want a nose job, a herr do an' a Joan Collins froak."

"Tae think it's only a couple o' days till we'll no be votin' in the Euro election."

"Ah'm jist tryin' tae calculate whit wid happen tae Maggie's itinerary if she had a six hoor delay at every airport."

"How many times have Ah tae tell ye it's no' Les Dawson that's runnin' the economy, it's Nigel Lawson."

"Ah think it's a man sayin' Mrs Thatcher's up the pole, Andra."

"The very idea has left ma budgie speechless."

"Efter a', Ye'eve got tae demonstrate aboot somethin', sure ye huv."

"Actually, I'm looking for something Japanese which I can refuse to buy."

"Ah've decided that Joey's tae be deputy leader in this house!"

"I must warn you, young lady, I shall lie about my age."

"Keepin' up wi' current trends, Ah suppose."

"Ah think they should jist leave Stanley Baldwin tae cairry oan!"

"Me and Norman would leave the Conservatives tomorrow if it wasn't for the fact that we'd miss the cheese and wine parties."

"Excuse me, son, Ah think ye've got a document leakin'."

"Could this I.M.F. crowd no jist gie us the len' o' a loan?"

"Funny i'ntit. Efter ten years o' Maggie the wife begins tae seem no' such a bad auld stick."

"Ownin' yer ain cooncil hoose jist means ye get flung oot fur no' payin' yer mortgage instead o' no' payin' yer rent."

"Ah canny understand why we need tae pay watter rates, can you, Mrs McClafferty?"

"Ma sister in Edinburgh's thinkin' aboot daein' the same!"

"OK so we live aff the Social Security! Whit's up, dae ye no' want tae feel socially secure?"

"Before they took purchase tax off an' put oan V.A.T., how much mare would it have been less than it wis before they put purchase tax oan in the first place?"

"He's that tired efter his day of action the doactor has gave him a week aff his work."

"A rent strike disnae mean ye've tae strike the Rent collector!"

"Is it true the Queen canny go tae Moscow because Maggie's got a world monopoly in red carpets?"

"The video o' which party conference are we puttin' on fur laughs the night?"

"Aye he really should watch his diet."

"Nice tae see Dennis standin' up tae her at last."

"Good luck with your butter mountain negotiations, old man."

"That's whit a' ca' colour discrimination!"

"Basically, I see it as a no way grass roots devolution situation referendumwise at this point in time, prima-rily."

"And of course your money will be refunded in the event of the devolution bill not getting through."

"Actually, Hamish is a sort of S.N.P. wet."

"She is expected, however, tae address them all as 'Hey you!.'"

"Ah say we should huv a referendum tae decide whether we should huv a referendum!"

"Complications, John — Nancy wants to restrict the number of Mrs Gorbachev's dresses."

"The way things is goin' here, Pakistan'll soon be hoatchin' wi' British bus conductors."

BOX CLEVER

In the beginning it was easy, of course. There was just one channel on the box, and whatever showed up on it was okay, so everybody just sat there.

It had its crudities, of course, because practically everything was shot live, and during a play you might see one of the actors rushing on hands and knees to the next scene, with his bottom playing a bit part right on the screen. I miss those innocent delights.

For some of us it was obsessional. The story is probably true of the incurable shoplifter who didn't actually want the shops he lifted, but did it to get his face on the box.

And we may recall that when there was a two-day power cut in an American city the birth-rate went up 50 per-cent. We live in a society where sex is a telly-substitute. And far from killing the art of conversation as earnest people feared, it has turned us all into compulsive blethers.

I can well remember, in pre-history, that the mere sight of a microphone, never mind a TV camera, would strike the average citizen totally dumb. Stick up a mike and a camera today and you'll get trampled underfoot by people who see their big chance for stardom. They all want to be Derek Jameson. Unfortunately, some of them are.

It was considered a scruffy taste at first, and well-bred citizens were careful to avoid it and leave it to the lower orders while they themselves played bridge or had high-level conversations about Kafka. In some cases, of course, their rejection of the box may have been part of the fur-coat-and-nae-drawers syndrome. But they surrendered when they started to discover that they hadn't a clue what people were talking about on the 8.15 train, because the only thing people talked about was last night's telly.

Strife reared its ugly head when we suddenly had more than one programme, and families split down the middle over which one to goggle at. Well, we discovered the answer to that. Get two tellies. I've got three, see!

And then colour, colour. Oh, you were nobody if you didn't

have colour. But just a minute. A wily manufacturer started selling perspex sheets for sticking over the screen, blue at the top, skin-coloured in the middle and earth-coloured at the bottom. Magic, as long as the screen never showed anything except outdoor scenes in Arizona. A studio shot with Gilbert Harding could look a bit funny.

Leave that to history. We're all polychromatic now and up to the ears in VCRs foreby so that we can record ITV programmes and play them back skipping through the commercials, including commercials for VCRs. We can get wee toty sets that strap on like wristwatches so that the drug is always available, and the Taiwanese are working on a system that sprays the picture on your eyeballs so that you can watch it in your sleep. Maybe a different picture for each eye.

You hate the idea? Just wait till these stuck-up next door neighbours get it. You can't let them look down their noses at you; though when their eyes are covered with *Bonanza* it'll be hard to tell where they're squinting.

"Pu' the blinds, Wullie, it's too nice a night tae be sittin' watchin' the telly!"

"Haw, Wullie, here's a novelty, somebody bein'
interviewed that husnae wrote a book."

"If ye've nae washin' they let ye play a video o' a washin'."

"Ye widnae expect a man ca'd Sir William Rees-Mogg tae be an expert in sex an' violence, sure ye widnae?

"My husband here has kindly volunteered to watch late into the night for anything pornographic."

"Is there such an organisation as Tellyholics Anonymous, Brian?"

"We must be able to compete with the increasing competition from television."

"Before the flamin' telly we jist had tae make wur ain sex an' violence."

"Terrible, i'ntit, four letter words on Channel Four Hivven help us on Channel Twenty-Five when cable Telly starts."

"Naw, hen, ah huvnae read the book but Ah've saw video recordin' o' the film made fae the play aboot th' book."

'It's wan lot o' bad news efter anither an' that's jist *Coronation Street*."

"Ah still say it's ma night fur the remote control."

"I think it's very good o' Mr Wogan givin' up three nights a week tae entertain us."

"Me an' him used tae fa' oot aboot whit programme tae watch ..... Noo we fa' oot aboot whit video recordin' o' whit programme tae watch."

"Ah widnae fancy playin' fitba' seven thousan' feet above sea level, wid you, Elsie?"

"We huvnae got a big dish, how about wur eighteen piece tea set?"

"It's jist anither o' thae soap operas."

"That's you at your best, watchin' Kung Fu hauf fu'!"

THE ME-AN'-YOU

There was a time in Glasgow when eating out meant having your mammy fling a jeely piece down to you in the back court. If it was unwrapped and landed in a puddle, that merely added to the flavour, and some keelie weans, having absorbed homeopathic doses of germs, grew up immune to practically everything.

There was the occasional wild outbreak, like shopping in the toon, when my mother took me into an actual restaurant for dinner (whoever started calling dinner lunch?). That could be a bit frightening because she was convinced everybody was looking at her, and if I raised my voice above a whisper she would shush me and blush.

I inherited that. When I started working in town and occasionally had to go to a restaurant for lunch, I mean dinner, I always took a book so that I didn't have to look at anybody.

It all seems weird now. By the time we had weans we were frightfully sophisticated and even had serious discussions with the waiter about the wine list, doubtless talking total rubbish. And our weans were the gilded children of fortune, absolutely brash.

There was one occasion in Number 10 Sauchiehall Street when headwaiter Louis asked the boy, then seven, what he fancied as a vegetable. "I fancy a bean," said the brat. Louis, a man of humour and spirit arrived with a big plate, lifted off the cover and revealed a single bean. The boy said thank you, picked up a knife and fork and proceeded to slice the thing. Louis gave up.

The boy's generation takes the whole restaurant thing for granted. They specify rare steaks, though I am downmarket enough to think that well-done steaks are rerr. They are right into the Italian and the French and the Chinky and they look people right in the face as if that was normal.

The very phrase wine-drinker used to indicate an antisocial degenerate. Now they blether about Chianti and hock and Chablis the way we used to blether about black-striped balls and buttermilk dainties.

Luckily we still have our wee misadventures to keep life interesting. There was the time my wife ordered chicken Kiev and cut it open to find the inside oozing blood because it had been taken straight from the deep-freeze and basted for a few seconds in the oven. Kiev right enough. It did look like something from Chernobyl.

It's still possible to sit at a table and discover it's under some kind of boycott. It's still possible to dig into a chicken leg and see it skiting across the room. It's still possible to shake a sauce bottle in vain and then suddenly cover the tablecloth with the stuff. (The trick then, by the way, is to glare at a waitress and say, "Look what you made me do!")

Oh yes, life away from home has disasters round every corner. But we're brave, and stupid, and we swallow them all. Except chicken Kiev, of course.

"That's nice, we're invited tae a cheese, wine and Rennies evening."

"An' remember, we didnae huv a fish supper, we had
an Italian carry-oot."

"Whit's this then, meals on wheels?"

"Terrible rid neck! She ordered scampi in the basket an' then complained the basket wis tough!"

"Basically, me an' Alec prefer the Chinese doon the road, their chips is better."

"We asked fur mints wi' wur coffee no' mince!"

"Whit will ye use for soup if the water workers go on strike?"

"Brother McCallum will now address the haggis which has been duly tested for salmonella, nutritional value and fat content."

"Ah'll huv mine fae a continent where they get sausage, bacon, egg an' tamata!"

"Compliments tae the chef an' congratulations on his skill wi' the tin opener."

"That's a wan cheeken supper, wan pizza, wan hoat pie, wan sausage supper, wan bag a creesps. Doesn't naebody want a blaady feesha supper?"

"Well, ye'll jist huv tae go BACK fur the chopsticks, won't ye?"

"The only thing that sticks in ma throat's the flamin' price."

"Haw, Guiseppe, gee us a poke o' thae silicone chips that they're a' talkin' aboot."

"Ah've saw on the telly aboot the world's starvin' millions but ah never expected tae be wan o' them."

"Ah wid never huv came if Ah had knew that their barbecue wis only fish suppers oan the back green!"

"Yiz'll huv tae wait a wee while folks, he's daein' cream of mushroom soup, beef stroganoff followed by crêpe susette, coffee, biscuits an' cheese."

"Whit dae yiz want fur sterters, wan wi' Sodium Glutamate an' Ribonulectide or wan wi' Hexamethylenetetramine?"

KELVINSIDE SYNDROME

Once upon a time, there were wally closes, and doors with cheeny haunles. A Glasgow family could dine out on those, even if they had holes in the waxcloth. I realise that in revealing such sociological entities, whatever an entity may be, I am setting myself in a particular level of society, fairly near the bottom.

Very well. I am such a snob that I don't care if people know I fought my way up from stanks and gutters to your actual sandstone semi-detached in your actual West End. Some of us conceal our origins, and we try to conceal Uncle Wullie, who has been known to overdo the Eldorado and, when provoked, will deliberately split an infinitive. My openness on that subject is, of course, arrogant snobbery. There is no snobbery in Glesca? Aw, come oan, get aff, Jimmy. We live on it.

So I can admit that I was born up a non-wally close, though we did, I confess, have an indoor cludgie. That was big superior stuff, my friends. In quite recent history, the closet on the stair was standard. A new insurance man from England chapped on the door of one and was answered by a small female voice. He asked if her mother was in, and she replied, "Naw, but she'll be in as soon as ah come oot."

The city of total equality is a myth as good as a mile. People raised in the Sooth Side never, but never, migrate to the West End, because they know that West Enders are psychotics in funny clothes. West Enders, some of whom have crept in from Parkheid after a crash course in pronunciation, regard the Sooth Side as a foreign land occupied by creatures that outer space got tired of.

To be honest, Kelvinside is not what it was. It has been invaded by human beings, a thing that traditional residents would never have believed possible. And secretly, some of the originals look longingly at Whittingehame Drive as an escape destination, except that it is too damned dear.

Ah, but a moment, a moment. The North side of Whittingehame Drive is enormous villas. The South side is bungalows. We may be sure that there are no windae-hings across the street. North is North and South is South, and ne'er the twain shall chat.

Does Springboig still look on Budhill as a social outcast? When I was pally with lassies who lived in both, I could never tell the difference, but they could enlighten me, often in a high-pitched scream.

We could always identify a scruff, because he said you and me, instead of you and I. Like, between you and I and the gatepost. I once pointed out on radio since the preposition (eh?) had more than two objects, we should say *among* you and I and the gatepost. I got a lot of protest mail claiming that I should have said "me". None of it was from Kelvingside, of course. The Kelvinside ethos, what's left of it, knows that "me" is a rude word.

Don't worry. The Kelvinside ethos may have been diluted a bit and even spread to the Sooth Side. But it is mercifully still with us, to maintain the innate superiority of the Real People. I am just acquiring double-glazed windows to sicken my neighbours.

Hivvings. Is it possible that double glazing is a scruff passion? Will I have to change my name and sneak back to the Gallowgate? Not on your life. I can't tolerate the lower orders, no' even a wee toty bit.

"Actually, we just want a pair to fix on our roof-rack from time to time!"

"Actually, Ah've got plenty o' hair but Ah suit the toupee better."

"Awfu' nice Agnes! Nane o' yer simulatit rubbish there ..... real rabbit if Ah ever seen it."

"Actually, that's a late ninteenth century ventilator."

"Of course, our air-conditioned colour T.V. has double glazing and deep-freeze combined!"

"I wish to order one of those satellite aerial dishes, preferably in Wedgewood."

"Don't you agree that the quality of life in Giffnock is vastly superior to that in Newton Mearns, Fiona?"

"Trust her tae go wan better! Ma boy came doon in five highers but her yin had tae come doon in six!"

"It's easy ... jist tuck yer frock intae the bottom o' yer knickers."

"Last year I wouldn't allow Hamish to buy me a mink coat, this year I'm not allowing him to buy me an Aston Martin."

"That yin'll no' worry the Animal Rights people wi' her alleged fur jaicket."

"Should anybody ask, we're cruising this year and there's no need to mention the Kyles of Bute."

"Norman would like to visit Dallas but I want to go to Dynasty."

"An' here's me, a' the road fae Glesca, thinkin' it wis a Sinatra recital!"

"Will this be the same Pavarotti that used tae huv the wee chip shoap doon Glebe Street, Andra?"

"I feel dreadfully sorry for any poor soul who doesn't have a mink coat in this weather, don't you, Fiona?"

"We're not sending Christmas cards this year and we're putting a notice in the paper warning our friends that we're not putting a greetings notice in the paper."

"Actually, Norman was a yuppie in the ninteen fifties."

AH, YOUTH!

These little things are sent to try us, as the co-accused in the dock muttered to his pal when the jury-box filled up with midgets.

We don't need midgets or lilliputians. We've got kids. When they're young, they greet a lot, maybe because they wish they were big. They poke their fingers into things, have you ever noticed? In our childhood, we never did that. We were perfect, as indeed we are today. We never licked the top of the sauce bottle, we never failed to scrub our necks, we never pinched the bum of the wee lassie next door.

The evil habits of the young are a totally new phenomenon in history. There was no teenage nonsense in Roman times. There were no outrageous fashions like the mini-skirt – remember the mini-skirt? (Keep the heid, keep the heid.)

Well, Roman legions wore togas, and they had mini-skirts, but that was only to keep the minds of their enemies off their spears. I suppose it worked. But that was in the cause of Empire-building, and when you're building an Empire, or a Pavilion, anything goes.

In this day and age, young people are rebels. Their parents never were. Their parents did as they were bid, they went to cafes and had the odd ice-cream – with raspberry, if they felt like breaking out – took a lassie home as a matter of duty in case there were savage Scotch terriers about, and maybe kissed her pinkie at the door because it still had some raspberry on it.

Today, they fling their weight about, the spoiled brats. They actually cuddle one another, a practice we must condemn because we're not getting much of it.

They wear funny outfits, some of which leave their ankles naked – a sight guaranteed to inflame illicit passions, especially among sexagenarians, and I apologise for the first syllable of that word. They go in for weird music, when their parents know that popular music stopped with Rose Marie.

And they play it on weird machines, when a caw-the-haunle would be perfectly adequate. That gramophone weighed half a ton as well, and it would be good exercise for the lazy young louts.

They also stoop to sipping lager at the infantile age of 18. ("You sipped lager when you were 18, Daddy." "Just shut up, I was more 18 than you are!")

They drop out. They don't drop off the edge of the world, which would be okay, though the Martians would kick up hell. They just drop out, they develop pony tails and whiskers, and they blether about the free society, which means they want lager for nothing.

They are just impossible. If we say we survived our teens on a diet of porridge and a twelve-hour day, some of the worst of them stand up and stare down at our dandruff and say it didn't do much for us.

The Berlin Wall is just a wee hedge compared to the barrier between the young and the mature. We will never understand one another, the way our generation understood its parents, and got bored to death with the dreary fogeys (I didn't mean that, honestly).

The sad thing about youth, of course, is that it goes away. No, come to think of it, that can't happen too soon.

"Please Miss, this is the second year Ah've been Joseph an' Ah'm runnin' the risk o' bein' type-cast."

"Ah think it's an insult tae us big weans that they
should ca' thae politicians a bunch o' big weans."

"Do try to understand, Fiona. The freezer was empty and , after all, they eat horse meat in France!"

"Ye canny win, sure ye canny? 50p fur an aerosol an' then remembered ah canny write!"

"Ah bet ye my dad's got a bigger mortgage than your dad."

"Dad, are ye a coloured person when ye go purple wi' rage or green wi' envy?"

"Ma dad says we learn tae subtract so we can coont wur darts score."

"We'll maybe need anaesthetic tae get a blazer oan tae this wan."

"An octuplets! That's murder! It's bad enough huvin' weans!"

"She'll huv nae trouble wi' the pedals, she's been ridin' a bike fur years!"

"Eat up that scampi or ye'll no get nae meringue glace!"

"Goin' tae the ordinary picturs disnae interest him since he has saw thae sex fims at school!"

Ah always thought heavy rock came fae Blackpool or oot a quarry."

"Ah don't know aboot you, but Ah feel like a flamin' eejit."

"Ma Toammy goes tae a selective school – the judge selected it fur him!"

"How much is the Halley's Comics, mister?"

"Please, Sir, we don't believe in uniforms, we a' want tae wear denims and tee-shirts."

"Ye shouldnae say 'this is Whit Monday', ye should say 'Whit Monday is this?'!"

"Ma complaint is that yer flamin' teacher went an' hit him back!"

"Although we do it regularly every year, William, I don't think we should refer to do it as a soap."

"See pressure, see hassle, Ah wid be better never fur tae huv went tae the flamin' University."

"Speakin' as head o' the English Department Ah object tae this yin Baker tellin' us how fur tae learn the weans their lessons an' that."

"I'm writing to the papers defending our educational system and by the way, Charles, how do you spell 'illiteracy'?"

"Mine's is rotten an' bad tempered but Ah widnae ca' he revolting."

"How are we goin' tae manage withoot the sex education?"

"He's goin' tae be an entrepreneur wance he's learnt tae spell it."

"Said ma herr wis the wrang shade o' pink."

"It takes that yin an hour tae make hersel' scruffy enough tae go oot."

"Beads is rerr an' trendy, sure they are, Wullie. Even the lassies is wearin' them!"

"Ah widnae work fur any guy that wis stupid enough tae gie ME a joab."

"Credit cards, my son, were invented so that ye don't have tae live within yer means."

"He's jist turned fifteen so this'll be his first season as a fitba' hooligan!"

"Ah never thought Ah'd see onything shorter than yer faither's temper!"

"Jist sherpen the spikes."

SEE THE PRICES?

Aye, we could just about manage on the wages if we didn't eat. A very expensive fouter, that stomach bit. Not sure if I should have used that word fouter, though my very respectable mother used it all the time to describe shopping. Etymologists among you, and there must be at least two and a half, are aware that it comes from Latin and old French and Old English and has wild sexual connotations.

Well, it takes the mind off the shops for a second, so it can't be all bad.

They are at us, you know. We have all been sucked into the supermarkets, and the supermarkets have the curious delusion that their purpose in life is to make money.

Their real purpose in life is to feed me for fourpence a week, but they have a psychotic fixation on money. And they plot it, we discover.

They have computers, which are crazy about money as well, and give instructions to keep moving the nice, cheap stuff, like half-carrots and single green beans, to different places every few weeks, so that the baffled customer has to traipse through unfamiliar aisles stuffed with the big profit items.

Full-sized chocolate Bentleys, time-share schemes in Beirut, Hebridean islands, that kind of thing. And as they know well, we are impulse buyers. If there's a time-share in Beirut staring at us in the face, we just have to have it, and maybe lend it to Auntie Teenie, since we don't actually need it.

Some of us, of course, view shops as a necessary evil, we know what we want, we scoosh out, shutting our eyes to chocolate Bentleys though we are tempted, but we just wanted a book of matches, used if necessary.

For others, the shop is the great social occasion, the talking-shop. They don't have a wee list with them, they have their eyes and ears and mouths, and they are fascinated by what other people buy, so they get home wondering if Tabasco sauce will go nice on a jeely piece.

They go in for panic-buying as well. If somebody mutters that salt may get scarce, they stagger home with enough to convert Katrine into the Dead Sea, and then have to panic-buy the house next door to store the stuff.

The wee shops can be more fun than the big stores. Fishmongers tend to be sociable people with the gift of the gab, though you shouldn't shake hands with them if your chillblains bother you.

And butchers can be fun, especially if they make their own Lorne sausages. I have an American daughter who never goes back there without a two-pound block of Lorne, which is unknown in the land of the free. It's illegal, of course, but she kids she's daft.

And do you know you can't buy dried peas in California? They have to eke out their miserable existence totally deprived of pea brae, the sowls.

One sinister thing is the emergence of the credit cards, of course. Glaswegians who would never have owed a tosser to anybody flash the things at the checkout with their eyes shut, and a trolley carrying 90 kilograms of edible trash. I can remember when the week's messages for a family of eight could go into a wee poke.

Oh well, I suppose that's why I weigh only three ounces now, and can get by on an ant's egg every four days. But I've noticed some smashing watches in Buchanan Street, and my wrist is itching. It already has three watches on it, but maybe I need one that shows Moscow time as well.

And I've had these shoes for nearly three weeks. I should be ashamed of myself. Ach, let's go daft, and not let the assistants die of loneliness.

"If it's no' up in price whit's wrang wi' it?"

"Funny how the sheep always wear their skin ootside-in, i'ntit."

"Fancy that! We jist dry wur tumblers wi' the dish cloth!"

"At the risk o' causin' a slick aff the Costa Brava Ah'll take a bottle o' yer sun-tan ile."

"A pair of wide bottom slacks for Madame!"

"Ah widnae fancy stickin' ma heid in wan o' thae tae get a perm, wid you Agnes?"

"Ah don't want nuthin', ah'm jist in tae complain aboot prices!"

"Everybody outside! There's going to be a price explosion!"

"She's either goin' fur a bus or tryin' tae keep up wi' inflation!"

"Things is that dear nooadays shop-liftin' almost feels like stealin'."

"Honest, Ah don't know whit tae shoplift fur their Christmas this year!"

"Thur puffball skirts is rerr an' handy fur the shopliftin' Isa."

"Dampt disgrace that! Ah've a guid mind tae take ma shopliftin' elsewhere."

"Agnes, if Ah wis tae knock off a tin o' John West wid that be salmon poachin'?"

"Ah don't fancy an F registered Porche, dae you Agnes"

"I know it's instant so why can't they slow it down and make it cheaper?"

"Hauf a pun' o' non-stick ham tae go wi' ma non-stick frying pan!"

"Funny, i'ntit, naebody seems tae get Salmonella fae salmon."

"Naw, we huvnae a perr o' toy boys."

"No thanks, hen, ah'm buyin' only British."

"Huv yiz ony fur ingrowin' toenails?"

"Ye want tae know the time! Well, Ah'll tell ye the flamin' time .... It's time Ah wis away fur ma flamin' coffee break!"

"Our prices huv went up because o' the nurses we huv tae employ tae render first aid tae the people who faint when they see how much wur prices have went up."

"Excuse me, hen, is this the end o' the spring sale, the summer sale or the start o' the autumn sale?"

"Excuse me, dae ye mind if Ah break up the Semmit Conference?"

"Ah think this weather's a sales racket promoted by the thermal underwear people."

"Why can Ah no', huv ma Christmas present oot o' Fraser's in Buchanan Street the same as you?"

"Ah always leave the wife's present tae the last in the hope that they'll be selt oot."

"Haw, Michelle, at whit point in time dae we start smilin' at customers on the run up tae Christmas?"

"Ah knew we wis visitin' the City Centre, Ah didnae think we wis buyin' it."

"Maybe ye'll be able tae get wan, Agnes."

"Five quid! Listen son, it's wan Christmas tree Ah'm buyin' no' Nottingham bleedin' Forest."

"Have you one to fit a micro wave oven thet size?"

"I wonder if I could have it sent."

"He's no' very fond o' Christmas shoppin."

"Ah told ye thae slip-ons wis too big for ye!"

"Are ye sure yer legs wis that length when ye brung the troosers in?"

"How much is that in litres an' kilometres if Ah'm only oot fur twenty minutes?"

"See that self-drive car? Well, it disnae!"

"Listen, Jimmy, if Ah knew a' the answers Ah'd be in flamin' *Mastermind*, woudn't Ah?"

"I'm afraid we can't help with your cash flow problem and suggest you contact your plumber."

"Ah'm away in tae buy some stamps afore they go up in price."

"She went window shoppin' an' came back wi' six windows."

"See the price o' claes! Nae wonder there's a' this nudity!"

"Ah suppose it could be worse, it could be a sex supermarket."

"Could ye gie me some o' thae strong pounds we hear aboot ....thur yins Ah've got are no' worth a damn."

"Terrible nooadays, i'ntit .... Bunnet made in Austria, jaicket in Hong Kong, troosers in India an' shoes in South Korea."

"Awfu' sad time the Autumn, i'ntit, whit wi' fallin' leaves an' risin' prices!"

"Ye get 10% aff the next 20% increase."

"Ah want wan o' thae new wave lengths."

AWAY FROM IT ALL

There is probably a future for Bellshill and maybe even Castlemilk, if they can tart up their boozers a wee bit (and certainly, Charlie McGlumpher, one of Bellshill's most enthusiastic boozers, could do with a bit of tarting up.)

Reverting to Charlie, you must know the tale of the Taiwanese tourist in Bellshill who had learned the patter, and accosted a passerby asking, "Where's the nearest boozer, mac?" Charlie, for it is always he, drew himself up to his full four feet ten and replied, "You are speaking to him, Charlie."

You think I am joking. Well, you think I am trying to joke, and failing. But I am now being deadly solemn, and I am good at that. It is all in a state of flux.

Time was when we automatically went to Majorca; and when I say automatically I mean that somebody pressed the starter button and we went into automatic control and wakened up somewhere in the Mediterranean with our shoes and socks off, our trousers rolled up to the knees, and our pre-programmed lips mouthing "Dos Bacardis, por favor, el noo!"

That was so much more sophisticated, so much more upper-crust, than the traditions of our ancestors, who went doon the Clyde, had a look at the paddle steamer's engines, and fell down the gangway at scruffy places like Dunoon or Rothesay and wore white sannies as they combed the area for haufs and haufs.

Okay, nothing wrong with Majorca or Benidorm. Well, not a lot wrong, apart from the daft teenagers smashed out of their skulls and a lot of people barking in German. There is a future for such experiences, for people with strong stomachs and crash helmets.

There are minor traumas, of course, like spending three weeks out of a fortnight's holiday sleeping on airport floors. For some dauntless travellers, that's the holiday, and to hell with Benidorm. You get better chat on airport floors than in Benidorm, and you don't get a lot of sunburn.

And if you ever get to Majorca, of course, you can slowly

realise that everybody, but everybody, from Fordneuk Street is there at the same time, so there is no chance of going home and talking about the film stars you met on your Continental trip, because the only people you met were the folk from the next close. They hate that as well, don't worry.

Actually, and leaving aside Bellshill and Castlemilk (you must be grateful for that), it can be somewhat more cheerful to slip down the Clyde as your remote ancestors did, fetching up at Largs, with its fabulous beach of enormous chuckies, which helped to finish off the Norsemen at the Battle of Largs, which gave rise to Nardini's and totally altered British civilisation.

There are very few airport floors on the way to Largs, or Girvan, unless you take your own with you. Hey, maybe that is the new status symbol! Portable airport floors. The Millport ferry will charge you extra for them, I fear.

So in our near future we shall have two distinct groups of holidaymakers: the traditionals, who fancy the Mediterranean, whatever the terrors; and the new, thrusting generation who have discovered strange exotic places doon the watter.

Bellshill and Castlemilk are waiting in the queue. But learn Taiwanese, for God's sake. You don't want to sound like an illiterate tourist.

"Harder, Wullie! Row harder!"

"This is mair like the summer we know an' love i'ntit,
hen?"

"Isn't ma hair a mess on that photy?"

"Are you sure you've got clean underclothes on, dear,
in case the plane crashes?"

"See the hot weather .... Ah'm nearly away tae a greasy spot."

"They don't seem tae cater much fur anybody that fancies a holiday in the rain."

"Ye've went an' came on the wrang bus! This yin's no' fur Portugal it's fur Port Glasgow!"

"Turn that radio doon – yer faither canny hear himsel' eatin' his crisps!"

"Aye Ah hear they're expectin' trouble fae Spanish holidaymakers in Dunoon an' Ro'say this year."

"Ma wife woudnae enjoy her fortnight in Rothesay if she couldnae moan a' the time aboot there bein' nuthin' tae dae!"

"Fur hivvens sake don't shout 'shoot', Wullie, in case ye're misunderstood."

"Jings, Agnes, it's jist a single-decker."

'Ah'm no' sure, missus, but Ah think ye wid maybe huv tae change at Carstairs."

"Ah always thought they had the waltz's in Venice and the oary boats in Vienna."

"Ah've got that many butterflies in ma stomach Ah could flee tae Majorca withoot an airyplane."

"Ah don't ever remember sittin' in an airport fur six hours on the way tae Rothesay."

"Book us intae the hotel nearest the European wine lake."

"On yer way tae Aberdeen, Wullie, d'ye think ye could drap the wife an' me aff at Blackpool?"

"How much if Ah get the bed an' he gets the breakfast."

"Jist think whit we must be savin' noo by no' goin' fur a month tae the South o' France!"

"If ma mother in Bellshill had a bedroom wi' private bath, balcony an' seaview we could huv went there."

"It's fae oor Isa, 'enjoying our holiday in Glasgow Airport, wish you was here."

"Makin' wan o' thae video nasties, Jimmy?"

"The health week disnae apply when we're in Majorca, does it, Wullie?"

"A think Ah fancy one o' thae self-catering holidays this year."

"Here we are in Torremolinos an' you keep moanin' aboot the rerr terr we could be huvin' at Rothesay."

"A' he's got tae declare is fower empty duty free bottles."

"Remember yon cruise we didnae go on last year? Well, we're no' goin' on a different wan this year!"

"Fantastic holiday! We had sunstroke, skinned noses, hangovers an' gyppo tummy an' that wis jist in Millport!"

"We've booked a wee cottage doon the Clyde this year overlookin' the concrete oil platforms!"

"Rerr holiday, but that wee Spanish waiter Ah fell in love wi' twenty-five years ago has got awfu' auld lookin'."

"Ah thought ye came here tae re-charge yer batteries no' tae top them up."

"Hey, Jimmy, Ah hope ye've read this, Jimmy."

"Ye should never huv wrote 'wish you were here'!"

"Ah didnae know this is whit they meant by balcony an' private bath."

"Has naebody telt them aboot Benidorm?"

"Listen, mate, if you knew ma wife's cookin' ye widnae recommend a self-caterin' holiday."

"Aye, we've went an' cancelled wur holidays in Spain an' we're goin' tae the Costa Brava instead."

"Ye begin tae weary fur an inch or two o' snaw, sure ye dae."

"The wife tells me we've had terrible weather fur wur holidays!"

"How is it Ah'm the wan wi the see through blouse but you're the wan they whistle at?"

"Depends whit ye fancy, in Spain they pinch yer handbag in Italy they pinch yer bottom."

"Seein' we're on holiday we'll look fur a bingo hall wi' a nice sea view!"

"Never mind whit the white paper says aboot goin' in tae Europe, we're goin' in tae Millport as usual!"

"Ah went through tae the Edinburgh Festival fur an hour an' a hauf yesterday but Ah didnae like it."

"Ah think Ah'm deveopin' jet-lag an' we huvnae even took off yet."

"We usually come tae Rothesay when we're on strike –
when we're on holiday we go tae Majorca!"

"Apart fae the Golden Road tae Samarkand whit else
dae ye recommend?"

"An' there wis this Spanish waiter that kept tryin' tae
get aff wi' me!"

"When ye booked a continental holiday did ye no' think
aboot askin' whit continent it was?"

"It wid happen jist when me an' Jimmie wis thinkin' aboot goin' oan a world cruise."

"Whit right huv they tae deprive us o' wur airport delays, Spanish tummy an' sunstroke?"

"How many times huv Ah tae tell ye, wur holidays wis a coach tour no' a hurl in the bus?"

"Ah've stood here since a week past oan Saturday waitin' fur the watter tae come up tae ma knees an' noo ye tell me the Mediterranean's tideless!"

"The Bellshill bus will be delayed ten meenutes because o' a strike by Yugoslavian air traffic controllers."

"Wi' a' due respect, Ruby, Ah don't think ye should cry yersel' an air hostess jist because ye got a joab blawin up tyres."

"Stop moanin' .... No' many people are lucky enough tae get desert rash, Spanish tummy an' sunstroke at Troon."

"If Ah had knew the world wis this size ah wid never had went an' came on the dampt cruise."

"OK ah promise no' tae go tae ony o' the gemmes .....Ah'll jist fight in the pubs an' that."

"Do Ah save mare money no' goin' tae Greece than Ah do no' goin tae Majorca?"

"Naw, it wis built fur last years festival an' we decided tae keep it on."

"Ah always come tae places where ye canny drink the watter."

"How dae ye expect tae wind doon if ye sit there sleepin' a' the time?"

"Efter a', you widnae like tae be pressurised by the media when ye're skiin' in the Alps, wid ye Agnes?"

"Listen! Ye're no' goin' tae the picturs an' yer no' goin' tae yer gran's fur Easter, ye're goin' tae flamin' Benidorm."

"Ye wanted a self-caterin' holiday an' ye've got it! Ah cater for maself an' you cater for yourself."

"Ah think Ah've went an' came in wi' ma platforms oan."

"Look up the Spanish fur 'where's the nearest Chinese cairry-oot'."

"Could ye please direct me to the nearest mountain!"

"If the Lord had wanted us tae go abroad for wur holidays we wid huv been born wi' a perr o' wings an' sun specs."

"Ah don't care if ye won the flamin' boat race, son, ye'll jist huv tae hing aboot wi' the rest o' them."

"This sun-tan ile's magic, Linda, the rain jist rins aff ye."

"Ah think it's a disgrace the way Lady Di shows aff her legs in public, dae you no' Michelle?"

"Fantastic! This holiday includes tips. We didnae get nae tips last year!"

SEE MATRIMONY?

There goes more to marriage than four bare legs to bed, of course. There's the cooking and washing up and cleaning the windows and going the messages, as husbands quickly discover; though, if they're lucky the wife will sometimes lend a hand.

Oh yes, we have to work at it, and sometimes work on each other's nerves as well. One of the problems is that a couple get interested in each other at an age when the blood is boiling through the arteries and the opposite sex is a magical mystery promising a lifetime of undiluted passion and even the odd cuddle.

Nothing wrong with that. But some wives get genuine headaches, apart from those who *are* genuine headaches. Few have the brutal honesty of the American lady who turned aside her man's amorous advances with the words, "Not tonight, Elmer – I'm too tired to think of somebody."

Men can have their faults too, improbable as that sounds. Having adopted the role of clean-cut Hollywood star during courtship, they are capable of relaxing into their true characters after the big event and do natural things, like picking their noses or their toenails or anything else within reach.

Young lovers contemplating a whole lifetime together sometimes have faint nagging worries, like what on earth they'll have left to talk about after twenty or thirty years. These fears are misplaced, of course. They will always be able to say, "It's your turn to go down to the midden, Jimmy." And of course they can always talk about the neighbours. That's why it's useful to have at least a couple of obnoxious neighbours. They stimulate more discussion than the nice ones.

Then there's money, of course, or sometimes there isn't. That can keep the blethering going, no bother. In earlier days, when pay-pokes were in more common use, some husbands were proud to take theirs home and hand them to the Boss unopened. That was just a cunning way of washing their hands of the horrors of budgeting, taking their booze money gratefully and leaving the wife with the headache (another headache!).

One hesitates to say that some husbands are capable of looking with excessive interest at other women. That is the cross some wives have to bear, but some of them have eyes as well. And come on, a bloke can't love a wife unless he sort of fancies the female sex in general. Not a bad excuse, that. Take a note of it.

One hesitates also to go into the subject of in-laws, unless one has a handy close to jouk up. But they do exist and can be a source of endless hilarity. There are, it's true, wives who can't actually die laughing at the antics of a mother-in-law, though they wish they could, or that she could.

But all in all, marriage is a fascinating state, which is why we often get into a state about it. And in that state, we never stop learning. We would like to stop, maybe. Forget it. But don't forget the wife's birthday. What's that date again...?

"Trust you tae buy a box o' crackers wi' paper hats that don't match ma frock."

"Ah don't know whit's happened tae yer mother, she went tae get something out the deep freeze half an hour ago."

"Dae you realise it's only bein' a teetoatlar an' no' huvin a motor caur that's keepin ye oot the nick?"

"Never mind the love-forty, jist get on wi' paperin' the ceilin'."

"Ah don't know whit fur people need a penthouse, can they no' keep their pent an' turps under the bed like everybody else."

"An' will you be able tae support ma daughter in the manner tae which she has been kiddin' you oan she is accustomed?"

"When Ah took you Ah didnae know ye were stereophonic!"

"Come to think o' it, Ah'm no' sure whether he said Ah was redundant or jist repugnant."

"Looks as if we're goin' tae be yuppies, Kevin."

"Ye realise, of course, that if we gave it up we'd be liable tae live an extra twenty borin' years."

"It's time me an' you had a productivity agreement!"

"Whit d'ye mean ye're a don't know?"

"Ever fancy a home computer, Walter?"

"Ah still say ye could huv got a job when ye left the school in 1946 if ye had been anxious!"

"Don't look now, Tommy, but yer happy hour has jist lasted ten meenutes."

"Naw, Ah don't fancy leisure."

"This diet's gettin' monotonous, we had grouse on the twelth o' August last year as well!"

"But surely, if America and Russia can agree to talk –"

"He's no' worried aboot radio activity it's normal activity that scares the life oot o' him."

"Me an' him don't huv rows noo, we huv confrontations."

"When ah wis a beauty queen thirty year ago Ah said ma ambition wis tae be a big, fat housewife in Bellshill an' it came true!"

"He's been huvin' workin' breakfasts since before they were inventit."

"See the price o' fags! Ah've had tae stoap the wife eatin' sweeties!"

"She's no' in, she's away gettin' divorced."

"An' don't come runnin' back tae me if yer mother' telly breaks down."

"Now remember tae tell everybody we've got oil fired central heating!"

"Wullie, can runnin' intae a lamp post gie a radiator grill metal fatigue?"

"See this joab creation. He created somethin' terrible when they offered him a joab!"

"An' tae think that when Ah wis Miss Coatbrig' 1961 my ambition wis tae be a top class model, huv ma ain boutique, own a string o' racehorses an' cruise roon the world."

"Awfu' thoughtful ma man – got me the len' o' a bunch artificial flooers fur ma birthday."

"Ye wisnae even wur first foot because ye wis cairrit hame heid first"

"He wis diggin' a shelter fae fall-out an' he fell in."

"Is this whit ye ca' a honeymoon cruise.... a day return fae Largs tae Millport?"

"Considerin' Ah've never took a bath by masel' Ah'm no likely tae be takin' wan wi' you!"

"Ah married wan o' them."

"It's a dose o' National Service yiz is needin'.... Look whit it did fur yer old man."

"Ah widnae fancy bein' Miss World, wid you, Agnes?"

"Your dinner is in the supermarket, go and buy it."

"You forget that yon time Ah kissed ye under the mistletoe Ah was also under the influence!"

"Ah think that yin's tryin' tae get rid o' her man – she keeps buyin' him fags!"

"He's absolutely dreadin' the 1990 year o' culture."

"She wants tae pay the Poll Tax an' Ah don't."

"If men wis oan V.A.T. you'd be zero rated."

"OK don't tell me! Ye've been panic buyin' again!"

"Naw, Ah'm lookin' for something for ma man."

"He wis lightin' the candles on the cake an' his breath caught fire!"

"Ah must admit he likes a drink but he's no' a womaniser."

"Ye must admit that's a lovely valentine Ah made ye send me."

"Actually he drinks it tae get empty bottles fur his hame-made wine."

"Whit flamin' use is a G registered the day when them next door got wan yesterday?"

"An' when Ah ask ye a question don't keep sayin' 'pass'."

"That's that yin's third man ..... A case o' Bridescake Revisited."

"Ah suppose this is whit ye ca' an Economic Semmit."

"When Ah fancied a bottle o' bubbly fur ma birthday Ah didnae mean a bottle o' washin' up flamin' liquid."

"He had an energy crisis before the the rest o' the world thought aboot it!"

"Ah object tae us women bein' looked upon as mere sex symbols."

"Ah'm hopin' tae get away wi' hauf price fur this yin."

"A love affair ootside marriage! Ah don't even huv a love affair inside marriage."